PORCHED HOPES

Credits
Editor, Brian Harris
Assistant editor, Tara Smith
Pagination expert, Jason Wilson
and a special thanks to Mark Tabor-Pascal

To the life never lived

PORCHED HOPES

H Stewart

Relic of a Known

Farn from reaction
I do disclose
The placent action
The heeded know
In all that varies
The wind bitters the rain
Chills the calming
Blanketing my know
To decipher
This rigid break
My thoughts negate
The unease of days
My wander
My window of distain
I field the coming
Calming days
While waiting
I work
Festering
The only in which I lurk
I seed acceptance
A linear linger
I smell you on the rain
In all of this
The man suffers himself
For the obligatory obligations
Of an October sailed away
From this the rest seeds me
Under my oak
I am shielded
From this reign
Until the break of unsparing days
We wander
In cadence of relay
So simmered I rest
From the tire of my ways

Longing
In that
Which haunts
The hidden
Relic of a Known

The Autumn Inside Me

And the sun will rise on his own fail
And hail down on all which is August
Steaming from the break of wane
Fighting for forget
Of the cooling days of your fall
The Autumn inside me
So withered
By vibrant rest
That a man can't help but wander
To days and ways ahead
And bask in all that was...
Still
And the world is still
In all
There is much
Muster
what is muttered by your stare
Be hold
Every breaking breath
Heed
The scent of roses running by
Listen
Laughter can occur in the help in us
Be
For what is I more than me
Care for that is all
The was
Still is
Remember
As
That
Is
Will
Tremble
Tremble
Is the should

Of Years

Where are you dear friend
Where are you hiding
Amidst the flowers of Spring
Or in the burnt grasses of harvest
Are you set amongst the stars
Cast against the darkness of an unknown
Or in the rising sun
Breaking the wane
Waking the world
Where are you old friend
Are you the brink
The poised we settled for
Or the wind
Are you the chimes that prove an invisible force
Or the hand
The comfort easing this descent
Where are you lost friend
Are you the mourning bird's rise
So settled on the first song being yours
Or the last light peaking through the eyes of the old
Where are you once friend
I hear you in my stories told
Of the once upon
The remembered glance
I see you in their smiles
Your reflection
In these tears
Your glimmering salt
Faded by the lack of years
Can you hear me friend
You always could
The lost eyes
Stark lips
Reminisce
There you are old friend
Immortalized in stone

Etched out
A reminder
We were not always alone
Your resting's peace
Minds us
We are all everywhere
Alone

Pulp

As dayless as my eyes
This shatter seams
No coming
No came
Less
A season's storm
Breaking my branches
Threatening my core
I have seen too many stumps upon this forest's floor
To become but a memory of a tree
Though I see more than leaves beneath me
After this season's storm
Years have caused me to no longer bend
Straight I stand
Now I may only look to my fallen hands
There is no mend in this
Only more space to grow
I branch out in many more spaces
My reach almost threatening the sky
Though these parts of me I see
Could brave no more
The death of a time
There is no funeral in this
No reflection of somber whys
Just my passing stare
Wear
Be that what it is
The ache lingers there
Only new rain will ease it in compare
The speckled light between my branches
Dances upon the forest floor
As it has and will it glistens
Light's reflection in an invisible mirror
Reflecting now on pieces of once self
As if on the constant grasses
Remains still are

As the pulp which forms this paper
Comes from more than fallen branches
I know the reason for those stumps
And I am honored that they are there
For without my fallen form
Where would I eye my stare
My wear has been but that
My eyed shatter
My seams

Pluck

To my trite and unenveiled time
I require
The average state of sensibility
I demand
Those hours of inspire so sought in my constants
Remember as thou breaks
A mosaic of matter compels the worth
Of the still continuing of the constant end
Can one but divulge the hours
Of still leaves and gray skies
Kissing white clouds
Is it fair and equitous
To paint the picture of the passed by
Or is there virtue in secret
To give the gained
May cause loss
And care is the seed of unhappiness
Somehow worth every salted smile
Is
Is as should
Trembling
To envelope one's self in the tire of know
The gleam of budding days
So shallowed by one's depth
May one walk as lightly as I tread
Thou I ask
In my summers set
Seed of harvest planted
Pluck

In Regard to Autumn

The force within fade
Is the require of mirrors
The latent litany of days
The passing of time
In regard to Autumn
You think of winter
And then to Spring
In this summer I sit
So weighted by heat
That I forget to look
To red leaves and burnt grasses
In regret
I bare
The familiar constants of my owned
Deedless
Still gaining trust
In one's property
My always owned
Neighboring the world
with warm cookies for the cooling of day
One
The finality of times
The numbering of years
To settle into accomplishment and acquire
So the divulge of the long seemed sate
When once again One
When the before and the behind are but this
To pass the time
As late evenings with good wine
For the familiar of self
Is so feared
That we bury it into an unknown
Somehow always knowing...
In the settle we see the rise
Reach for evening in afternoon always

Quieting the screams of aging
With the wisdom
Of One

Hi

And as one calms
It cools
The seeping of years
My unrighted say
Here there is no deserve
The passing of knowledge is lighter
Than the walk with one wise
So throught
By a once kingdomed desire
We wilt as we bloom
The never in knowing
Teaches the passing
The mourning bird's song
So in glee
Searching through mourning's mist
For the cadence of its song
A companion
The melody of days
The humming of streets
The creek of chairs
The sitting and the rising of man
The work in steps
The coming and going
All the passing byes
In our hurried hopes we find heed
The sparse clouds
A coming storm
Our pouring...
Drinks
The empire built on empowering
Coffee
Tea
Variety
Still he sings.
The melody of days

As we listen to one another's says'
The glide in flight
Carries us farther
Than flapping the of wings
Higher
Our hellos
The passing high

Crossed Streets

So sept are the sins
Of honest times and coming men
That one could but cross
The crowds of forever
For time
The decadence
Inside
Still graves of shallow memories
The decide
I deem your hours as crossed streets
The blinked by
The accidentally seen
Broken man
I mend you not
A woman tired and calm
Looks to the see
To this I remember
The screen looked through
My penitence of being
Share not my memory
Call not to my confines
My riddle is but truth
Come to call

Rightless Widow

My rightless widow
Still complains
Of placent days
Where one wept
In thought of ability
The requite of reverence
Her smile
So longed in familiarity
So placed
In all her walls
A life spent
Laying all the bricks and stones of home
Her mortarless castle
Seeking the bind
She swears
Will never tie her together
Her fear of foundations
So spent on a place
Her placent so
Her temporary prosper
Until she runs
From the permanence of that mortar
The mark in one so strong
That weakens the fortress
Of a fiend
Less relent
The cement
Which waters her weathered
Stone may cause no crumble
But break the lone
And a creation
So pinned in soft thought
That only
A swear of maligant majesty
Will reap her sowed

Watching her
Turn her prison into a home
A recipe for a rocket
Waiting
To explode
Her sparkle captured in the night sky
By every painter passing by
My love
Will widow this day
Eyeing the glass
Her familiar look away
For that I sit and eat and try not to say
Thank you
For my foundation
Found
In your fortress of relay

Alongside Another's

Dream now
Sweet forgotten
For the time will surely come
In which to ponder hope
We all have our distances
We all have our pain
Listen in all ways
You will sleep
Digesting words
Like soup filled with meat
Its warmth bringing you life
While too much or less as stale
In the end leaving you weak
Rise now
And begin the day with one's owned
Form you solidity before you seek
Love
I will drive fear into your heart
Like a knife left alongside another's path
Love
I will sneak up behind you
And hold your hand
Hate
Comes from love misserved
Like soup brought to you on a plate

Brightened Blade

The sun has set
As it will rise...
The sky hints
Sprinkling its gray...
Upon us
This...
The green seems brighter
Against the cement...
This sit
My bade of days...
Regardless of the distance acquired
One Requires
The same as home...
Your shade
Is your strength...
The stretch of one's redemption
To let go...
Is a stronger drink
Than one... bears
Bourbon's burden
Is as bright as the cement
We The Grasses...
To the pave of our day
That aid to our travel
The sidewalks
Streets
The veins of our city
To that which countries team
I toast
Till our burdens meet

Still Captures

The surface of a mind
My wither
Stretched across the horizon
As a dawning
At night
The circumference of one's hope
Charmed by the intertwined
The focus
Weathered by light
And smoke
Still captures
The cuts into the virgin sky
The colors of signs
A space within
One's mine
Those who walk have risen
Weather withered by walk, wonder, or standing steps.
There pace stakes the same
Travel of mine mind
This time
Our reality of commonality
A separate space
Is our wade
Ankles or knees
That which envelopes
Is our tread
My singular
Wintering
Our fall in between
The wind of our summers
And the rest one needs
Regardless of season
I found sanctuary in leaves
While drowning in heat
This the film

That August leaves

Upstream

My how I have walked thru your valleys
And avoided your mountains
Only to climb the trees which comb your view
My reverie
Feet wading upstream
To find the chill in your daze
Every peak closer to your why
High enough I have seen you grow
To the acquire of constant snows
I stare across from my separate fate
From my constant Christmas
To your sun soaked snows
And I sight what I see
All in which we have grown to be

Veining Hepatic
"Into my death"

A fevered state
Meant's dormant day
When only the numbing of one's possible
Weighs upon my heart
The channel to my beat
Exposed
My pressured pulse leaks
And one tends
To this merciless state
By pouring all the possible negate
Unto there flesh
Poisoning a wound
As if to challenge fate
All the while
Trying to kill the dying
Younged by a fate
Running toward the light that has
Always dimmed me
Proclaiming Distain
Of beauty
And one walks
We wait
To give in to given negate
To all of our Narcissistic neglect
Sating ourselves with knowing
Of the one we have disallowed
In all our living
Life

My Never Failing

The continued pouring
A trickle of time
Reigning down
On the set of a summer's storm
Wide out and choked
By the perception of size
The reflection of self
Under the daze of days
In that I will
My smile focused on the dawnless horizon
My Never Failing
With every drop in this pour
Meager means
So sent
Of shadows casted by light

Trinkets of Trying

To my ward
I wander
In a vagrance meant
I so divulge the days
Weighted by me
And I whittle away my fallen branches
Carving belief
From death
Tiny objects for one's mantled peace
That knife held in hand
A command
The tiny trinkets of trying
After the gone of dawn
One sits and fumbles
Between dried leaves
To make something
From dying heed
The need to carve one's remains
Into belief
Is as idle
As life passing

On Overflowing

I once left
Thrice
I wept
For the return of a nevered land
My home
So foiled
Castle of resolve
Calls
The possessless say
On counters of faith
One places plates and mugs
Jars of flour for cakes
Things hoped
Things make it seem like home
My feel
Is not like a place
My comfort has no contain
My heart leaps from my chest
Threatening my bones to break
There is no box
Chest or cabinet
That shelves the well inside
Just other plates, cups and mugs
Left overflowing
On counters

A Call for Class

Rise not thy fears
Forth a favored forever
Seamed by distress
Naked in means
Left aside the resolve of stood
Are not the roses fielded
As there crept gates rust
Rise not thy fears
Formed by length
Proceed to thy presence
Hoped
Tilting memories
Has

Library of Means

To that I fold
My days filling in the iridescent
My believe
Tired by the mortuary of my remains
The neighbor of my dream
I harden
My Settle throught
My permanence penned
By my soaring flatulence
I know my lies
My counter of truth
The damning of one's self
For the lack of belief or love
In one's own meant
Which self shelves my days
In my library of means
Stacks of empty and unread books
Lighted by freshly dusted windows
Come in
Rest
Read
Stay
We might just build an again
Until one washes the windows
through which they peer, they may
only look out by standing close to the light,
while looking in is first a far away task only
a dim and clouded reflection
will be the worth seen.
My days spent dusting
Will only be seen
By those who find intrigue
In things kept clean
So I will call no maid
Or servant from my past

I will just sit
While feathering away my own clouds
I will watch
As the sun fades the binds of my books
And I will draw curtains at night
While listening for the knocking
The coming to say
My what a beautiful place
Is it alright if I
Come in for a stay

Windbreaker

May my cease not become your eyes
Focused on years
I fell not to your
I disguise my offer
My strength fallen to fortune
Aye my belief
Withered
Rest so sated sleep
Smiles meet
For my once
I imagine your strength
Shoulder me dream
For I will be the stand that breaks your wind
For my faith I stare
Farn from compare
I seep meet
Your pulsing belief
That aye
That seek
Sought in my

Silent Ship

Aye aye, my friend
Aye I
To the see
We brought together
Through windows of we
The stern breaking waves
Through endless sees
To beached seek
Past by the vessels
The afloat
The remains of once
Scavenging with spirit of hope
Antiqued antiquities
Covered in barnacles
Belief in need
Aye aye, my stranger
Silent ship in the night
Your might be as looming
As the evening itself
The smell of salt
Stings our eyes
Kept wide in watch and wonder
As you tread along your way
Aye aye, my captain
Your fists of front fathered me
Brought me to display
The flag of my ship born
Colors of my birth
Causing fear in sum
As it breaks against the winds of docked days
Aye the see itself
Cold and causeless
Sought by vessels built
To sake and cause the wave
The buoys afloat
Near cannons fell

The splash of one's sunken swim
Without the vessels fallen and afloat
Aye as distilled
As the drink of a sailor
Come home from the see

The Wild Rest

Was not the world
Of kindled sorts
Of ways fighting familiar
Dreams destined for soil
The seed in need of cover
Weight to warm
The darkness chanced
Was not the wild
For tame's sake
To plow unto the unforgiven
A muster of years dampened
Rain allowing quench
Was not the living
For dying's sake
Tormented unto teams
Bound together by the rough
The vagrant and the seen
Where is not the world
In hours spent
Inside fallacies
Mortal means
The gain left unreplied
How not the wild rest
When not the living wake
Was not the world amongst
Was the world not need

My Once

You looked good that every night
I eyed
My darkness gleams
Inside
That which is yours
Aye
Same familiar loss
In the star you have become
My once
Always
Reminder of remain
Until
Until
Eying the darkened blue
Deepening your smile
I love not the hate you serve
You who is served inside
Forgotten

Wander of Will

Nor sad but learned
I leaned
Against for now
Sake itself
I resolve
To that
Starless sought
A pression of pen
No longer poised
You sent me sake
Toward the wander of will
Carve against me
The paper
The substance in which carve
Was
Is

Tabor

Mark
My witness
Unloved yet cared
I press less than loved
Him
More distant now
I serve the forgotten
I hate his pass of chance
Cleared by clouds of understanding
You who might will
Those whom still
Yes
Remain
Less the regard
Frames forgotten
Feeding self
With that which is plucked
From fields

Porchless

To rise
With less
And walk
To bade belief
Without lesson or accomplishment
Metaphors left
To remain without existence
Unpurposed continuance
The passing ache
Smiles
Within emptiness known
Inspired only by those surrounding
In life *lives* reason living

The Horseless Trader

For the sake
I sound the seem
My bellow of own
To thy create
I mount the horseless trader
To deem thy order of self
You my friend are the swallow
Of my soup
My create
Your perched chirp sounds my symbiance
Your chipper displays
The sake of sound
To thy trader
You deem my order
Your touch inspires my taste
You thy lover deepen the plate
You in held hands
Touch the taste of sound

Fruits for Foreign Fields

What are these things we have
Gathered here
Among the roses within the weeds
What are these things
We have kept here
Shadows unregarded
In streets sided by light
What are these things born here
Settled in left
The carriage of keys
Unkingdomed home
Where are these things we have
Kept here shelved
On under-bridged nights
Miles the distance
Ordering regard
Where are these things born here
When smile's might holds no more
When dreams birth the resurrection left incomplete
Where are these things we have
Gathered here
When good is only gained
The allowance of past
Voices forgotten
Strength
Less a whisper of love
What are these things we have
Gathered here
But fruits for foreign fields

Thy Recall

Listen lover
To my recall
Of nights when morning came
Twice I found
All the reasons for belief
In eyes swallowed by a sleepless hope
Disbelief
Dispelled my sleep
A nocturnal nature
Sighted by an unfamiliar wince
Of days
The ending known inside
I weep alongside you
Thank you for your smile
My fear has become
The rendition of our love

Pages

You my pen poised
My ink, my ache
Sullen by streetlamps
Contained by leaves
I remember stories so told
That whispers where the knowing
Words guide
They do not answer
They lead to the stumble
In our search
I would have never known
Without
Without
The lies to sate the truth
The kiss of the wind
A star perched underneath streetlamps
The edged stance
During quakes of love
My mighty held through and past seek
Thy unpretension
Nor calm or callous
Less...the beatitudes
A prayer maintained for another's truth
Within
Within
The hold worth not fighting
The chess in the park
Our heartbeats the timer
Between plays and practice games
I found no rest in winning
Checking my mate
You saked all beginnings
For the instant always so few give away
I bide
The withheld

Held me
As the suns setting lets go of the warming
Bringing the cold
Without care for the night
The worth within
The dimming of day
I design not property or purpose
Just a stumble along the world's way

A Mutter of my Requite

I dream not of your mastery
Or your honesty
But the lie beside you
Your taste left
To warm
The comfort of these years too few
I break
For not the fallacy
I live for not time
Wonderless ignite
I dream not of conquer or concur
But for sated smiles
Less the thought
For the aid of laughter
I poise now in my set
No resolve
Matter
Less a mutter of my requite
I call not to a lover
I dream not of a man
For my husbandry
I rest
For the thought sought in my reverie
...is but love

Make Me Listen

My love for you
Makes me listen
Fuels my remember
Of has not been
You are my should
Inspiration lost
Is found
In eyes cast upon smiles
In the less I feel
You are the success
In my failure
The decompression of fears
Loves let sees all
I could end in all
Or continue in me
But
Though
If
Us
Them more...
The strain of something
Is Else

My How We Listen

My how we listen
Between each other's screams
Mine louder than others
Your smile
Still covers
All the cold in my soul
Without knowing one warms
More than with
Though this stretches my porched hope
That in which I let go of
In the bustle of getting by
Our own why
Without it
The
The found they
A questioning
Of the regard of the regardless
Love simple things
The ease of day
The let loved
Has

Foreign Coins

Times left
Found
In foreign coins
Severed brought
Barring reflective minds
Islands of calm
Coming together for storms
Autumn
Regardless of leaves
Seeps pocketed change
I knew the value of your eyes lady
Before I could realize
The toss of your coin
You are all but spent my friend
A mint lost
Pressed paper unto metal
Coined in your gaze
You are a part of my change
For the sake of my keep
I lock you lady
Into my safe
Catalog you in my wealth
Insured, tax paid
I look for nothing to lean
You back no lone
You righted time
Found among foreign coins

Constant as Breath

The life I have seen, my friend
Is weary and weak
Together with left and long
Hope proceeding all disappointment
The life I have lived, my friend
Is sad, and pained
Apart in away
Of love shown and souls broken
For the crime of the unconditional
The life I have felt, my friend
Is full of ache and inspiration
Pride in the heart I was left
When all else lost
The love I remember, friend
Is the worth of years spent
It's dying
The memory of friends left shinning
The strange smile I have felt, friend
The room in which I sit, friend
Is empty
My taste left to warm my desperations desert
A hope for self...unknown
The thought of final demand denied
A tombstone carved from chalk
Before the rain
I sit my friend
I grow
For reasons unknown
The ache I have felt as constant as breath
My known of life
The no one standing in my shoulders greet
All for my nothing, friend
I tell you this

The Carrion of Dreams

There
Staring across the city
Its end comes to view
The talent and fortune gather
For its discomfort
They lie
In await
Inactive
They mutter in bars
Screams of variation
They cail in their apart
Our once
Favored
I will not bestow our excellence
In any other means
The joint reality
Our carrion of dreams
Envelope your loss
You are disgrace
A disappointment
Enough!
So little
You have no reason dor your pride
You are weak and diminished
You are set in your failure
THERE IS NOTHING INSIDE you
Look at what you have become
You mold yourself to them
YOU
ARE
NONEXISTENT

Held

To abstain
From breath
The inability to allow death
My masochism is being
Yet still I wander
Searchless
Seek no longer sates me
My fornis has but space
My soul inside this place
I know
I will not surrender
Though I remain without regard
Fevered and childless
Love left my fate
Leaving...
Terror in smiles
I surrender to break
I, the fallacy of sake
See no channel to water my fate
Virtue still gone from me
Given
The less of self
Is the more
The unpassioned refuse
I can no longer muster
Just
Step
Place to place
Nothing,...
I hold held
Death barter me for sake
I dizzy from days declareless

Home

For I seem
The terrible
Crossed
My stitch is time
That which in ways...
Unmeant
Gathers a wear
Aware
That which pines the poisoned
To crept corners
Shutters
Thine alone is my offer
My charity
To self
And sent
My remember
The comforts
Of that which remained uncomfortable

The Grave Await

In eyes
In flight
Terror teaming in days
Daffodils deeming
Love's grave wait
Ponder
Amidst
I am as fortuned as a kindling's kiss
Our rise
So soaked by ordinary joy
That dreams deploy our damnation
The fragrant foe
My familiar
Seems solemn and kept
By quiet dreams
You are my answer
Unpictured love
The rise of a choke
Breath to leave me soon
Ponder days
A memory of my shattered mirror
Left aside the street
Shards of left
Reflecting a world unbroken
Teaming with need
Left are the pictures captured in mirrors
Moments
Together sewn
Memories
The memorials built in our minds
To that which has past
The headstone of our hearts
In cemeteries of seams
Yesterday...
Death is as yesterday

Life
The space spent in between
The coming and the came
Now spent
Digging dreams

The Bradford Pair

Dear-refine the stars
Stab your forever with forks
Cut and carve
The seek
Climbed through
For elegance in means
Again
You strive for the forgotten leaves
Bloom ye not roses
But fruit
For substance
Cleared
Life in taste
Exposed in flowers of before
You my possible shark
Should wilt for the consume
Aye pies of pears
Dense sweet softened by time
To mold for ferment
Love come to me as blossom
Turn to thy fruit
And cast yourself for wine
Our ferment is but forever
Age upon the climb
Stage be the tree climbed for again
Tell me not of prune
Rain be our quench
Green leaves softening the trunk
Years for soon as now

Bloom

Bridled

Expect me to sleep
Arms uncovered
Promising you
Voiceless reason
Twilight anewed
Expect me to prosper
In your eyes
Unwondered realize
Lips looking up
Even when away
Expect me to listen
To the sound of mellowed days
Breaking for the spare
Unbridled for the rest
Sanctioned soon
Expect me to sin
Against the forgiven
Faultless in denial
Taming but inhibitions
Unmatched in best
Expect me to remember
Times when
Times again
Times sin
Expect me to whisper
Of days lost and found

Eshay!

There is more than the required here
Living amongst us
In shadows and in clout
The haze of
The unbecoming
Tints of tainted times
There is more than the desired here
Lost amongst forever
Shapes to warm the loss
Sun rising
For comfort of fears
Dreams of the awoken
There is more than the living walking near
Streets filled with ancestors
Clodding the clad of concise
Sparing the unforgiven
In sight
Of feel
There is more than the deserved here
Dedicating dreams
Along the desolate days which define destiny
The deedless claiming characters of plight
For pleasantries sought
Bye familiar
There is more than the known here
In knowledge's height
Gained forth a favored familiar
Less lost
For more

DeLoma

She to well up
Upon horizon's sent
From arch to answer
I walk
To her
Wallow in left
The regard of step
Simple prose
Told
Of unanswered
Wait
Until pass comes
Her of dreams stewed for spoiling
To march unremembered
I of innocence
Her of remark
Dreams to pass
Eyes unseen
Gentle beauties believe

The Garden

Hence the garden
Flowering with days ahead
Blooming with the inequities
That light and beauty pertain
Hence the garden
Left shadowed
In our winter
The wane waking
Death for order of life
Youth green glowing
Presence becoming fruit
The picked are consumed
Hence my garden
Ripped from lips
Tastes of subtle sweet wonder
For its rot
The linger of an early summer's taste
Hence the garden
To be tended
Weeds thrown
As ashes
Expelled by an unnatural wind
The exhale of existence
Thrown
Hence the garden grown
Remnants of planting
Of the known
My seeded reminder
My garden grown
To wither
Into the mulch of plant
A cycled seeding
Wince my garden
Hence the garden grows
In sun and night

Nurtured by light
Shown in the shadowless
When apparent left
Hence my garden
Hence my known
Giving what made this world grown

To Then

Time saked me in silence
Reverent known
Hour less requite
Thy transition honed
By thy clarity
The release
I wander
Set upon
Thine owned...
You friend
Smile at the lone
In break of sparing days
Thy song
Unsung for sang
We not require best
Fornate made
Lessening the listened to heard
Aye heart
Hear, Here

Cardinal

You thy red
But glide upon winds forgotten
Yet felt
My red
Walls creating stop
Aye, the symbolize
My cardinal
For you I strain my hear
Forth for song
Sung is but the cause
Of our afternoon's rise
The dawning of a late wake
Has but the sharp of you
Between the green
Settled on brown branches for chirp
The striking settle
Your ease pleases
But me
Dear bird set in red
Aye, my cardinal
Friend...

Tow Yard

The reverie
My excluded
Based upon familiar
Set in far apart
They gather
Without exchange
Placing heed in hand
Taking the remains of once
As a solid reminder of stood
Underneath gray skies
Behind gates
Cheapened by razor wire
In a hut a button is pressed
And the gates of a kingdom
Brought into Hell open
We enter
The man unaware
Of existences other than owned
Rattles the old truck
Leaving us alone
Only I could see the sept in my friend's smile
As the island of dead horses passed by
The view filmed
From an unkept window
No care put in the glance out
Staring through dirt and rust
Into the same
I remember
As the voice of cost rings behind my ears
The once in all
Regardless of yards towed

Permanent Poise

Aye, the cylinder stopped
The turn came to halt
Rusted rods
Clench
Beginning comes to end
Before
The scene saw
The crowd famished
By unfinish
No turn to come
Chains tightened
By push
The clock of halt
No free will break
No hint of grace
In this market's space
Poised for no sake
Struck
In wince
Thy clench

Little Girl Grown Down

I once saw a hope in your eyes
Little girl grown down
I once saw a smile appear
Behind legs looking out
I then had a know
Of the window in which you would peer
The salt of years has not weighted you
Little girl grown down
Stands now with force
Little girl we all need
Need comes from lack
You never gave up
I once saw a dream let go
Your seed acceptance
I once heard you scream
Little girl grown down
Trembles for trite testimony
Tears to come
You still laugh little girl
I first saw you worry
Little girl
The day you were born
Concerned by the troubled
Still so young
I now see a woman
Surrounding bright eyes
When bright eyes become big little girl
I know
The little girl grown down
Is staring back through
The lack
Into glass

Dance

Dance with me
For gods among angels
Are but man
A stance of arm pressed
For twirl
For life
I to be no god
But dance
Dance with me
For life is but a step
A dip
A curtsy
Till bow
Dance
Angels of man
Woman
Dance
Stand stepped to lead
To glide the silk away
Dance with me
For there is no other way
I bide
The forever of your stare
To light an evening with afternoon eyes
Cheek to chest
Rock
Thy hold
Dance with me
For men are but gods
Till Thou's create be love
Dance

Back to Deeds

Countryless is man
No color for cause
Still beat of day
Blood to pump
Again
Regardless of nation
Is but strength of wake
For chance to negate
But breath to days
Honour
Thy lips press
Tongue to kiss speak
Remember
For eyes cast on reason known
Silly reveal of day
Porched across earth
A heavens way
Be that our earth
Man to God again
All to stand for fall of fight
Bear not borders for less
Deeds to trust
Apprehension
Bloom to grow again
For fight be not fade
For days of step are marked by fall
Winter to season us all

Gillham Park Pool

So far we have come
To fall again to once
To return to the home
Of our mortar
To be but stance
To glide in step
Walk to wade
To bask in depths
Shallow float
Feet beneath
Miles of meter
Before the see's floor
Float
Back resting upon water
Face to sun for char
Glide with arms
Drink for quench
To see's of self
I do remark
In my matter
Of my tiny pool
In Gillham Park

Among Thorns

It could have been stranger days
You and I
Then
Among the roses
When they were thorns
And branches
We widdling within their points
It could have been longer
That we were together
Straining through the strange
You and I
It would have been the wind's gourge
If our lips had kissed
Drawn together by afford
Then
We of sin
Could have been
It could have been the color
Of every earth and hour
It could have been each other
Among the roses when
We together
Were thorns

Troost

The flesh of this suffice
Is longer now than the gutters
Rain's tendency to shimmer
Underneath streetlights
Plains the asphalt's grave
Below
Metered moments
I shark the swim of puddles poignant
To steadier shudder
The cold save
Of this sinning's sanctuary
Favor of the elements
Life still structured to rest
Above the cities lurk
I carve
Sincerities sins
Upon painless stakes
Of
Of

Je n'a pas de valeur

It is evident this evening
That my concept has been conquered
That my ill has become issue
To those inquiring eyes
It is my itinerary
To display nothing but the known
Je n'a pas de valeur

It is an apparent afternoon
And I am alone
It is much like forever now
The sun is hot, the stars are gone
It is my only operation now
You listen for low tides
Je n'a pas de valeur

The derelict of day dawns
It is morning now, again
And it's break
Basking before me
In it I know
Je n'a pas de valeur

I know mainly of midnight
Other times are often
Yet it is then
That I call to the sky
Black and adorn with stars
To speak of the moon
To spell out it's cause
For I know my own has past
And I worry not
Of any but it's cause
The moon
For I know
The hand which welds the tides

Long ago
Put I, to rest
And I understand
Much of many and morning
As well as afternoon and evening
Yet it is mid the night
That my answer lurks
Among stars I know
Je n'a pas de valeur

Often and Ordinary

It is often
That I am ordinary
It is a rare recluse
For I, or any to be abound the walls of inordinate
And somewhere inside
The wooden walls of want
Hides more
Within
The strange matter of my touch
Memory allows often to return
I am quite likely mad
I find this often, and ordinary

The wane of woe

I am weak with regret
For I have come again to love
And I am lost
In away
Unlike before
I am found
As a sensation
My body melded to mind
I depreciate
Every action
Inside the same remark
I am dying in love

Lost Letter
To Kansas City

Dear, I must forgive myself of love
I must replenish
The hard pressed lost
It is not that you are forgotten
It is not that we are alone
It is of I
This forgiveness
It is of my life
For you see darling
Time has past me once
Unto the favor of the gods
And I have fallen since
Because of you
At least this is what I have come to believe
After the winds of your breath threw against me
Words of hate and ill action

Dear, I must forgive myself of you
Not only now
But in forever
For we all have faults
And you have driven me into a valley of despair
For my own
And the raven of your push
Was filled with the sharks
Of this City
Island surrounded by nation
Here we have no waters to wash ourselves from the dirt

Dear, I must forgive myself of love
For it is blind and I did not see
The razors in your quick wit
Or the alleys of your claim
Avenues they were not, love
Their stench still stains my skin

So I must wash myself with the wind love
Time will surely grant me enough breeze
To become again

Dear, I must forgive myself of your light
For it was dim
And I dark
Have lightened
To the world I must go love, to the world I must shine
Your shadow has caused tears to turn to mold
For to long love
I have listened to others hearts
For to long love I have listened to your part
In the stories told
Love, I must forgive myself of you
For I as many must move on
Toward the insatiable rest
Toward peace love, I must go
And I will offer you no memory in mind, love
No memory harsh or unkind
I will not lurk in the yards of our past
Even on midnights alone
I must bury your memory in light love
And favor not this night which has turned to day
Yet still I place no shame upon my dawn
I just wake with neither gather or gained
To go on love...
To go on.

Porched Hopes

To me, this is us
Undriven by sense
Mellowed by moonlight
So to say so to say
For thus write
To me, this is us
Him standing there
From sit and rock from swing
For porch
Is our stance
We who are the was
Of evening's summers late
The air of regard
For drink
For me, this is us
Exhaling the in
In soft alone
We gather
For day to come
The soft of eve to grant
Our tone
Of day
Of left
Our throne
The cement block expelled from home
Here, this is us
Robed in hope

Welcome
Into my life

To end as gracefully
As the knowing
Questioned by those who understand
Won as solemn
Will shadowing
That which blinds us
Dimming gods for focus
In order to hold
Aye, remembered
Aye, fallacy of strength
Feeding the forgotten
A stone thrown upon the mound of once
But a marker for my cemetery
The yard of stood
No name shall you carve
Nor time
Please disregard place
For I call not to peace in death
I pray not for rest
Spread me upon the world
So that I can touch all that I missed
The sun itself
Cannot rise against a love as strong as I have found
Breathe me in as you wake
Aye, to become the air
Life
Be that my death
The legacy I leave
Choke upon me on cold days
Curse me in the rain
Allow me to cool you
Tickle your face
Let me dance among leaves
Wings flapping against me
In order to find a glide

Allow me
Regardless of temperature
To be breath
In my death

You Will Remain

Don't forget
I remember
The ways of those which have walked alone
Of harvested streets
And of seek
Of all inabilities meet
Don't forget
I remember
Those days of night and stars
Relish me begotten
For I remember
Don't forget
Child of beginning
Father of fortune
I remember
The forgotten
My kept
Yours unprisoned
By
Don't forget
I remember
How and who came
I to shiver
From my remember
You will remain

Blue Enough

And then
The loss was gone
Like clouds of the unforgiven
Sipping through the sky
Blue enough
To remind you of stars
Coming through the black of deep nigh
Dawn will be our answer
It is coming
Through
The loss of gone

ABOUT THE AUTHOR

H Stewart currently resides in the warehouse district
east of Kansas City's Crossroads Art District.
The book was writen in South Hyde Park, a section
of Midtown, Kansas City.

A preview of H Stewart's forthcoming release.

H Stewart's

The Unnecessary Flame

Long Since Dried

The smell was putrid
Insightful
And then art
As we exited
Entered
The back porch
Which was more of an exit
To the outside
She gave me this
The winner of less
For love the same
Still now as I write
I smell the paint
It has long since dried...
Money becomes the topic
Of conversation
No one involved
Has found sate
When it comes to bills
Charge me lover
Give me the energy of could
Let me know of my receipt
Astranged stranger
The smell was putrid
Insightful

On Once

On once
Round tabled Knights
They gathered for the relax of exchange
Mellowed by evenings of push...

Still staring
From visor black
He gleams from again
A knowing pulse
of this place

The one who smiles back
At me
Through his see
of saw and smile is he

Then there in the white hat
Holding on
To this smile..
his current cling

She
Wearing pink
The blond strown down
Smiles
Skinny lips drag
The smoke which clings
Round
Tabled knights

Thy Sept for the Same

There to be my romance
Shattered in a matter of maimed
Shards
Cast across
Streets paved for dreams
Remain be my let
Scattered in sit
To stare unto strown
As to the unto...
The pale glimmer of now
is but streaks
Of yellow
Orange cast
Gold
On streets lighted for change
In evening's come
For love...
Of again
Time to be the pallette of our remorse
Colors to splash
Piece to weld against forever
To create from the crumbles of again

The Shadow's Dream

I cannot dream
But to be
The silhouette in your eyes
But your arms' focus
Your hands' sure rest
The silence shared
I cannot dream
But to be
The laughter in your voice
I can call to no other fate
I can claim
No other intoxication
I cannot dream
But to be
Your rest
From a world un mighty
And pained
The press against the part
Of your place
That which calms your cool
I cannot dream
But to be
The rest of your sate
The curl in your lips
After good taste
A lady
But I try
Though I cannot find place
In any
As the silhouette in your eyes

Hymn

As the morning sun
So is your art
You
The part of rise
That causes colors
Forces purple
To scream of coming
Orange; Yellow; Blue;
Your eyes to cast
My shadow to light
That sparing bleak
Of evenings come
Again; Again;
Moonlight becomes bask
Twilight the throught of my knew
Of now
You dark staring blue
Come to me
As the morning sun is

A Remain of Let

For love to listen to me
Now
Would be obscure
Inactive
Pretentious
A remain of let
Has coiled itself
Inside my inhibitions
It has allowed
Any; Every; thing
That is the all
Inside
These white washed walls
My remember
Now the forget
Of Dark; Dinge; Dive
Some of this is the compel of reminisce...
Home
Here inside the wallow
Of let
Relax
Regard...
Accompanies the lost
Inside
Came to be quiet...
Dreams...
Stranger drinking with me

Thus Gaze

Let me think of love
The pure pastures of our relate
The two dozen dropping
Petals dried for floor

Let me think of love
The climb of stares
Your eyes to be my blue
The pool of my soak
My sink

Let me think of love
For times sure separate
The divulge of when
You and I...

Let me think of love
For pain's sure
Allows this drench
This sate

For now
I will think of love
The tick of seconds past
For moments
For days

Years to comes as
Gone
As love
For sure
Will stay
The measure
Of ours
Let me think of love
The cold wind

Whispering flakes
Upon my face
After hours of flight
Your green against the grey of day...

Let me think of love
The sate of my place
The arms spread for tuck
Head to shoulder
Back to bed
The dim of day

And I will think of love
In all ways
Our bodies curled to task
Laughter
The release of sum

Let me think of love
For hours come
In should's past
Let thus be the pour
Of rain
From which we huddle
And hide

Let me think of love
For in sure
There is nothing left
But the blinks of ways
And our spent
To say
Think of love...
Let thus be our gaze

"For Pile"

And so I have swept
The dust
From floor unbecoming
To wash with rotten mops
Un rinsed from before
And so I spread
The waste of again
Once more
I watch your tread
From mounds
Of dirt
From streets
Of ash
Clouding the air
Till settle
For pile
And drag
Up to barrel
For sit
Until dump
So the steps of honest and hindered men
Same be the struggle
Same be the wince
Of separate
The draw of line for entry
Unto
Floors freshly cleaned of dirt

"The Unnecessary Flame"

Light to Capture
Embers of remorse
To tell the story
Of the unnecessary flame
The kindling
Of possible ignite
Coals of come and gone
Day and night
Stones fortressing
Protecting the dug
From ground for hearth
Now to sit before it's warn
On dew ridden grasses
Smoke
Churning
In it's trickle up
To sky and face
For hand to see
The branch of tree
Fallen near flames
A char
To touch
The grasp
Limb to fallen limb
Now to use
It of bark and brim
Upon the inside of my pocket
Found
A once full sack
Staled from days away
To pick
Now from that bag torn
A marshmallow for warm

The Unnecessary Flame is "Porched Hopes" rebuttal.
It was written in September of 06.
While "Porched Hopes" took over three years to
compile, The Unnecessary Flame took only a few
days over 3 weeks. I hope you have enjoyed this
tiny taste. I leave you now with its release date.

H Stewart

"When September"

If ever there was anyone
But you
I would be
I would be
The star which set the moon to the right phase
On the wrong day
If ever there was...
Anyone
As true
I would be
I would be ...
The sea without salt
An ocean of you
And me
I would be
I would be ...
If ever there was anyone so new
Age would be lifted
Like skipping rocks
Like skipping rocks
Gliding home
I would be
I would be
If ever there was anyone
As you
I'd be the break of days
Bustin bottles over any say
But you
If ever there was
If ever there was
Anyone at all
I would be
I would be
Anyone of you
As true
As you

I would be
I would be
The sun settin up blindin dates
Our October
Till December
In November
When September
I would be
I would be
The breeze coming through
That screen between me and you
If ever there was...
I would be
The see of saw
The lookin up of down
I would be...
The smile
Of everyone
In awhile
Being
Right now

September 2008